HISTOROPEDIA
QUIZ
BOOK

AN *'Ask Me Questions'* BOOK

SHAUNA BURKE

GILL BOOKS

Gill Books
Hume Avenue
Park West
Dublin 12
www.gillbooks.ie

Gill Books is an imprint of M.H. Gill and Co.

Text © Shauna Burke 2017
Illustrations © Kathi 'Fatti' Burke 2017

978 07171 7574 1

Print origination by Jen Patton
Printed by CPI Group (UK) Ltd, CR0 4YY

This book is typeset in Brandon Grotesque and Wanderlust.

The paper used in this book comes from the wood pulp of managed forests. For every tree felled, at least one tree is planted, thereby renewing natural resources.

A CIP catalogue record for this book is available from the British Library.

5 4 3 2 1

About the Author

Shauna Burke is a full-time secondary school teacher from Co. Waterford. She teaches English and Religion in St Angela's Secondary School, where she was also a student! She studied English and Religious Education in Mater Dei Institute of Education and graduated in 2014. She has a passion for table quizzes, trivia and telling stories. She is also the sister and daughter of illustrator and author duo Fatti and John Burke!

QUESTIONS

Quiz

1

Round 1

1. What stringed instrument is Brian Boru thought to have played?

2. What was the most secure part of a Norman castle? a) the keep b) the tower c) the ramparts

3. Which of these was **NOT** one of the Penal Laws?
   a) Catholics and Protestants couldn't marry
   b) Catholics could not become hairdressers
   c) Catholics couldn't adopt orphans

4. The building where monks spent their time writing and decorating holy books was called a s_____.

5. Which army won the Battle of the Boyne: the Williamites or the Jacobites?

6. Crinoids are marine animals related to what five-pointed sea creature?

7. What did Fionn mac Cumhaill's wife dress him as to fool the giant Benandonner? a) a dog b) a baby c) a teddy bear

8. The G___ L____ was formed in 1893 to promote spoken Irish.

9. What type of houses were also called 'back-to-backs'? _____ houses.

10. True or false: In the 19th century, boys commonly wore dresses until they were six or seven.

Round 2

1. The coracle was one of the first types of what in Europe? a) bicycle b) boat c) car

2. The war fought between Irish chieftains and the English Army during the Elizabethan era was known as the _____ Years' War.

3. True or false: The King of Leinster invited the Vikings to Ireland to help him get his kingdom back.

4. Ancient Irish warriors preserved what body part of their enemies so that they could show them off?

5. What did the Mesolithic people **NOT** use to cover their tent-like shelters? a) thatch b) canvas c) animal hides.

6. Famine ships were also known as _____ ships, because so many people died on board.

7. What Munster county beat Louth in the first Gaelic football All-Ireland final?

8. On what day of the week did the Easter Rising take place?

9. Henry VIII ordered the closing of what across Ireland? a) schools b) hospitals c) monasteries

10. Which poet and academic became the president of Ireland in 2011?

Round 3

1. What is the name of the crescent-shaped collar made from thin sheets of gold worn during the Bronze Age? L___.

2. What first went on sale in 1944? a) staplers b) permanent markers c) ballpoint pens.

3. What sweet, sticky food was used to flavour meat dishes in the Celtic era?

4. Jerome O'Connor carved a statue of what famous Irish nationalist? Robert ___.

5. True or false: Countess Markievicz was sentenced to death for participating in the 1916 rising.

6. The Harland & Wolff shipyard where the *Titanic* was built is in which Irish city?

7. What is the name of the fungus that destroyed potato crops during the Great Famine? B___.

8. What stringed instrument was on the United Irishmen's flag?

9. How many Irish people were deported as slaves during Cromwell's conquest of Ireland? a) 10,000 b) 25,000 c) 50,000

10. Who was the UK's first female Prime Minister? Margaret _____.

Round 4

1. What type of animal was a Scelidosaurus?

2. Which of these shapes is **NOT** carved into the decorated stones at Newgrange, Knowth and Dowth? a) spirals b) zig-zags c) hexagons

3. A new version of what flag was made when Ireland joined the United Kingdom?

4. Daniel O'Connell is buried in G____ Cemetery in Dublin.

5. Jane Wilde, who was a writer for *The Nation* newspaper, was the mother of what famous writer?

6. James Connolly was born in: a) Scotland b) France c) Italy.

7. Bram Stoker was the author of what world-famous book about a spooky vampire?

8. Sir James Murray from Derry invented what medicine to relieve the Lord Lieutenant of Ireland of stomach pain?

9. What was Cúchulainn's name before he defeated Culann's hound? S____.

10. Approximately how many people worldwide were killed by the Black Death? a) 10 million b) 45 million c) 75 million

Round 5

1. The Ascendancy were the only people in Ireland who had the right to: a) farm land b) vote c) marry.

2. What college in Dublin did Robert Emmet attend?

3. Spell 'scriptorium'.

4. What war ended in 1975? The V_____ War.

5. Palladius was sent by the Pope in 431 to be Ireland's first b___.

6. Granuaile was the P_____ Queen of Mayo.

7. 'Vadrefjord' is the Norse name for which county?

8. When is St Brigid's Day?

9. In what decade was colour TV brought to Ireland?

10. Was William of Orange Catholic or Protestant?

Quiz
2

Round 1

1. John Lavery was a painter known for painting the symbol of Éire, which was used on: a) Irish postage stamps b) Irish coins c) Irish banknotes.

2. True or false: The Penal Laws were enforced for nearly 100 years.

3. The biggest defeat of English forces in Irish history is known as the Battle of the _____ Ford. Hint: It's a colour!

4. Who became 'more Irish than the Irish themselves'? The N_____.

5. There was a shortage of what knitting material because of the Black Death?

6. What type of bird were the Children of Lir turned into, according to legend?

7. What is the most famous passage tomb in Ireland, found in Co. Meath?

8. Fenians were members of the Fenian Brotherhood and the I_____ R_____ B_____.

9. Name the Irish circus company that started in 1888 and is one of the oldest continuously touring circuses in the world. F_____ Circus.

10. In what county was the GAA founded?

Round 2

1. Stirabout is a type of: a) hot drink b) watery porridge c) lumpy soup.

2. The United Irishmen wanted to break Ireland's connection with what country?

3. True or false: Éamon de Valera was both the Taoiseach and President of Ireland in his lifetime.

4. Those who did not support the 1921 treaty were called the _____.

5. How did Daniel O'Connell arrive at his meetings? a) on horseback b) on a bicycle c) in a carriage.

6. Y___ Ireland was a movement that involved Catholics and Protestants who wanted to bring about equality and wanted Ireland to have its own parliament.

7. How were the rooms inside a Norman castle lit?

8. In 1642 the Irish leaders decided that the Irish people had to obey the laws of King C___.

9. Anne Devlin, known for her bravery in the 1803 revolution, was Robert Emmet's: a) sister b) girlfriend c) housekeeper.

10. In 1918, what group of people was given the right to vote in Ireland?

Round 3

1. Sir Edward Carson was the leader of the Ulster V_____ F___.

2. What is the name of the mythological fairy woman who cries when someone dies?

3. What hill in Co. Meath is believed to have been the seat of the high king in Ireland?

4. What was the name of the strong honey drink favoured by the Vikings?

5. When a landowner in Co. Mayo was ignored and excluded by his community for refusing to reduce rents, what new word was introduced to the English language? B_____.

6. Who wrote the novels *Ulysses* and *A Portrait of the Artist as a Young Man*? J___ J___.

7. What Munster county did the Normans land in during their second invasion of 1170?

8. From what fish did Fionn mac Cumhaill gain his knowledge?

9. True or false: Daniel O'Connell did not support Robert Emmet's revolution of 1803.

10. What Irish show is the world's second-longest running talk show?

Round 4

1. Who began to settle in Ireland during the Iron Age? The C__.

2. The Battle of the B____ took place in 1690.

3. What did people call the illegal radio stations that appeared with the invention of radio? Hint: Shiver me timbers!

4. Hitting or slapping children in schools was made illegal in Ireland in: a) 1964 b) 1979 c) 1982.

5. In what county beginning with 'C' would you find Brownshill Dolmen, which has the largest capstone in Europe?

6. True or false: The Irish chieftains defeated the English at the Battle of Kinsale.

7. Which of the following was **NOT** on board the *Titanic*? a) a gym b) a basketball court c) dog kennels

8. John Philip Holland from Co. Clare is known for inventing the: a) hot air balloon b) kayak c) submarine.

9. What was the name of the small buildings that monks slept in?

10. Who arrived in Ireland in 1649 as the Lord Protector of Ireland to get revenge for how British settlers were treated? O_____ C____.

Round 5

1. The Irish Parliament called for volunteer soldiers to protect the country while the rest of the British troops were sent to fight in: a) North America b) South Africa c) Eastern Asia.

2. True or false: Almost 400,000 people emigrated during the Great Famine.

3. What was the name for the groups of huts built on stilts or man-made islands in a lake? C____.

4. A Mesolithic campsite with animal bones was found at Mount Sandel in which Ulster county?

5. On which mountains in Antrim did St Patrick mind sheep? S____ Mountains.

6. What was the flowery name of the civil war between York and Lancaster in 1455? War of the ____.

7. The decisive battle of the 1798 rebellion was fought at: a) Ketchup Hill b) Vinegar Hill c) Salty Hill.

8. Daniel O'Connell organised ____ meetings. Hint: They weren't as scary as they sound!

9. What poet, remembered as Ireland's 'national poet', wrote 'Down by the Salley Gardens' and 'The Lake Isle of Innisfree'? William ____ ____.

10. What was the type of armour worn by the Normans? C___ __.

Quiz

3

Round 1

1. Which came first, the sinking of the *Titanic* or the Great Famine?

2. What is the name of the enclosure surrounding the motte of a Norman castle?

3. What civil rights leader and activist was assassinated in 1968? Martin L___ K___ Jr.

4. What language did Granuaile and the Queen have to speak when they met? a) English b) Irish c) Latin

5. Daniel O'Connell founded the C___ Association, dedicated to bringing religious freedom to Ireland.

6. True or false: Third-class passengers on the *Titanic* were those closest to the lifeboats.

7. In the Stone Age, people lived in huts built of w___ and d___.

8. A cesspit was a Viking: a) bath b) toilet c) bed.

9. Who was the father of Oisín, who lived in Tír na nÓg?

10. Complete the famous phrase by Theobald Wolfe Tone: 'Many suffer so that someday all Irish people may know j___ and p___.'

Round 2

1. The famous GAA venue on Jones' Road in Dublin was named after Archbishop Thomas _____.

2. The walls built to separate Catholic and Protestant communities in towns in Northern Ireland are called _____ Lines.

3. You can visit a mass grave from the Great Famine in the town of Skibbereen in what county?

4. Who did Cromwell send to take his place in Ireland when he returned to England? a) his brother b) his second cousin c) his son-in-law

5. Who lived with Oisín in Tír na nÓg? a) Niamh b) Nora c) Nessa

6. In the 13th century, Irish men were noted for wearing _____ without a beard.

7. What 1916 Rising leader was a poet who established two schools which were dedicated to teaching children through Irish? P____ P_____.

8. What type of rock is used to decorate the wall in front of Newgrange? a) quartz b) marble c) basalt?

9. In Irish, which month is named after Lug, the god of harvest and light?

10. The Republic of Connacht, established in 1798, lasted for: a) 12 days b) 12 weeks c) 12 months.

Round 3

1. The remains of what now-extinct animal can be found in Dublin's National History Museum? Irish e___.

2. Granuaile (Gráinne Mhaol) means: a) bald Gráinne b) tall Gráinne c) ugly Gráinne.

3. True or false: Protestant workers, farmers and shopkeepers were considered part of the Ascendancy.

4. When William Gladstone's Home Rule Bill was defeated it caused serious riots in what Irish city?

5. What is the name for a storyteller in Irish?

6. Thomas MacDonagh commanded the Volunteers in J_____ biscuit factory during the 1916 Rising.

7. What metal is made when tin is added to copper?

8. What material was invented in 1907? a) cotton b) plastic c) rubber

9. True or false: Early Irish national schools had chairs with no backs on them.

10. The G_____ F_____ Agreement was signed in 1998 and signalled an end to the Troubles in Northern Ireland.

Round 4

1. Brian Boru is buried in what county in Ulster?

2. A St Brigid's Cross is said to protect your home from what?

3. Which of these is **NOT** a symptom of the bubonic plague? a) black boils b) vomiting blood c) hair loss

4. In which province was there a rebellion against English and Scottish settlers in 1641?

5. What metal was worn by the rich and powerful during the Bronze Age and was used to make ornaments and jewellery?

6. What college in Dublin was established in 1592?

7. Daniel O'Connell moved to France to study: a) medicine b) law c) education.

8. Seven Young Irelanders were taken to Van Diemen's Land, now part of Australia and known as T_____.

9. How many leaders of the Easter Rising were executed? a) 10 b) 16 c) 22

10. The *Book of Kells* and the *Book of Armagh* are examples of i_____ manuscripts.

Round 5

1. Dr Francis Rynd from Dublin invented a type of:
   a) plaster b) syringe c) thermometer.

2. True or false: The first bicycle was invented in Germany and had no pedals.

3. Which came first, the Battle of the Boyne or the Nine Years' War?

4. An Ichthyosaur was a large marine reptile, resembling what modern-day water mammal?

5. In the myth, Aengus fell in love with a woman called Caer, who turned into what bird every two years?

6. What Scandinavian country did the Vikings who raided Ireland come from?

7. Which king started the Tudor period in England? King _____ VII.

8. Oliver Cromwell wanted to have his portrait painted with '_____ and all'.

9. If a Catholic became a Protestant during the time of the Penal Laws, they were allowed to take:
   a) their neighbour's house b) their parents' land c) their brother's livestock.

10. A selkie is an Irish mythological creature that appears as what marine animal during the day?

Quiz 4

Round 1

1. The United Irishmen were a group inspired by the American and F_____ Revolutions.

2. Was Daniel O'Connell Catholic or Protestant?

3. In what year was the World Wide Web invented?
   a) 1989 b) 1995 c) 1971

4. Every child in school once had a tally stick which recorded the amount of times they: a) talked in class b) got a question wrong c) spoke in Irish.

5. What political party was founded in 1905 by Arthur Griffith? S___ F___.

6. John H___ and David T___ were awarded the Nobel Peace Prize in 1998 for their work in ending the Troubles in Northern Ireland.

7. It's believed that the traditional Irish harp may have come from: a) Spain b) Turkey c) Egypt.

8. Lilting, used instead of instruments to provide a beat for dancers, is also called '___ music'.

9. True or false: According to medieval Brehon Law, slaves could wear cloaks with only two colours.

10. High King Labraid Loingsech wanted to hide the fact that he had what type of ears?

Round 2

1. 1900 marked the death of which Irish playwright and novelist? Oscar _____.

2. Around what year did the first people come to Ireland? a) 6000 BC b) 8000 BC c) 4000 BC

3. Name the hole in the ground filled with water that could have been used for cooking meat or bathing during the Bronze Age.

4. What reptile is St Patrick said to have driven out of Ireland?

5. True or false: The lords and ladies slept in the upper portion of a Norman castle.

6. Grace O'Malley, the most feared pirate in Ireland, was better known by what name?

7. The few survivors of Cromwell's first attack were sent where to work as slaves? a) Barbados b) Jamaica c) The Bahamas

8. During the time of the Penal Laws, some Catholics sent their children to ____ schools, where children were taught in secret.

9. Rebel leaders from the 1798 Rebellion had their heads cut off and stuck on spikes in what town? W_____.

10. How much did the Catholic Association collect per month from its supporters? a) one penny b) sixpence c) one pound

Round 3

1. You can visit a famine ship in Dublin called the J_____ J_____.

2. What did Michael Davitt found in 1879, which organised protests against unfair rents, taxes and evictions?

3. Tipperary beat what Connacht county in the first hurling All-Ireland final?

4. What is the name of the Parliament of Ireland?

5. In what year was a ceasefire called between Loyalists and Nationalists in Northern Ireland?
a) 1981 b) 1997 c) 2000

6. The C_____ Brothers were an influential Irish folk group popular in the 1960s.

7. Name the games played in Ireland that are almost as old as the Olympic Games.

8. Sir James Martin, born in Co. Down, invented:
a) the ejector seat b) the telescope c) the cornflake.

9. What Irish airline was started in 1936?

10. Spell 'Neolithic'.

Round 4

1. What type of stone was mostly used by the Mesolithic people to make tools? a) basalt b) limestone c) flint

2. Badb was a Celtic goddess of war who was able to turn into what bird?

3. Ireland is known as 'the land of saints and _____'?

4. True or false: The Normans originally came from Denmark, Norway and Iceland.

5. What Leinster county was formerly named Queen's County by Queen Mary I?

6. Many earls had to go to Europe after the Battle of Kinsale. This was known as the ___ of the Earls.

7. The followers of William of Orange were called W_____.

8. During the time of the Penal Laws, the Volunteers were noted for their: a) unusual hairstyles b) colourful uniforms c) shiny boots.

9. What province benefited the most from the Act of Union, as lots of jobs were created?

10. How long did Daniel O'Connell spend in prison? a) three days b) three months c) three years

Round 5

1. What crop did poor people depend on in the time of the Great Famine?

2. True or false: The Fenian Brotherhood was set up in the United States.

3. Pádraig Pearse famously said '*tír gan teanga, tír gan anam*', which means 'a country without a _____ is a country without a soul'.

4. In what year did the *Titanic* sink? a) 1905 b) 1912 c) 1921

5. Who was the leader of the Irish Republican Army during the War of Independence?

6. George Bernard Shaw's play *Pygmalion* inspired the musical *My ___ Lady*.

7. Follies are strange buildings because: a) they had no doors b) they had no roof c) they had no real purpose.

8. What American president visited Ireland in 1963? J___ F. _____.

9. Name the type of knitted jumper that comes from Galway.

10. Who was Ireland's first president from Northern Ireland?

Quiz

5

Round 1

1. Which came first, the Iron Age or the Bronze Age?

2. What famous ship sank in 1912?

3. What type of megalithic tomb is Newgrange?

4. The Turoe Stone, an example of the La Tène style of art, was found in what Connacht county?

5. What statue, by sculptor John Henry Foley, is situated on O'Connell Street in Dublin?

6. In what room would the lord and lady of a Norman castle host dinner and watch minstrels perform? Great ___.

7. Caravels and galleys are types of: a) weapons b) boats c) shelters.

8. When Cromwell's son-in-law had captured most of Ireland, Irish Catholic landowners were told to go 'to Hell or to _____'.

9. True or false: Catholic bishops, priests, monks and nuns had to leave Ireland under the Penal Laws.

10. Samuel Nielson and Lord Edward Fitzgerald planned a rising in what Irish city for 23 May 1798?

Round 2

1. When Ireland joined the United Kingdom, they were ruled by a parliament in which English city?

2. Daniel O'Connell ran for an election held in what county?

3. Isaac Butt from Donegal started the H__ R__ League in 1873.

4. What GAA competition was first held in 1887?

5. Whose widow was elected as a TD in the First and Second Dála? a) Pádraig Pearse b) Thomas MacDonagh c) Thomas J. Clarke

6. Countess _____ was heavily involved in the 1916 Rising and was one of the first women in the world to hold a cabinet position.

7. Peig Sayers wrote her book *Peig* about life on which islands off Co. Kerry?

8. Evie Hone and Harry Clarke are both artists that are known for: a) marble statues b) stained glass c) wooden carvings.

9. Thomas Smith from Dublin invented what cream used for nappy rash and other skin problems?

10. What common vegetable can be found in colcannon, boxty and champ?

Round 3

1. What was the first canal built in Ireland?

2. In what year did World War I begin? a) 1918
    b) 1912 c) 1914

3. Was Megalosaurus a carnivore or a herbivore?

4. On which day every year is the inner chamber of
    Newgrange illuminated at sunrise?

5. What is the Irish name for a kingdom?

6. Which of these was **NOT** one of the purposes of
    a round tower? a) to call people to church b) to
    sleep in c) to hide in times of danger

7. Who introduced coinage to Ireland? a) the Celts
    b) the Vikings c) the Normans

8. What was another name for the bubonic plague?

9. Soldiers from what European country came to
    help the Irish chieftains in the Battle of Kinsale?

10. True or false: Oliver Cromwell made it against the
    law to celebrate Christmas.

Round 4

1. What harsh new laws were introduced to Ireland in 1695?

2. The leader of the United Irishmen was Theobald W___ T___.

3. Daniel O'Connell's final meeting was set to be held in: a) Clondalkin b) Clontarf c) Cork.

4. In what Munster county was the Irish tricolour flag first raised?

5. When did Conradh na Gaeilge succeed in introducing Irish into primary school classrooms? a) 1880 b) 1900 c) 1920

6. Éamonn Ceannt, one of the leaders of the 1916 Rising, was a talented player of which Irish instrument?

7. True or false: Michael Collins did not support the 1921 treaty.

8. Jonathan Swift wrote what book about tiny people on the island of Lilliput? _____ Travels.

9. What type of horse racing was invented in Ireland in the 18th century? a) steeplechasing b) flat racing c) endurance racing

10. Traditional flat caps, or 'Paddy caps', are made of what woollen fabric?

Round 5

1. Who was the first president of Ireland?

2. Spell 'Newgrange'.

3. Echinoids are a type of fossilised: a) sea horse b) sea urchin c) sea anemone.

4. What is the name for the large circular mound of a passage tomb? C____.

5. Brian Boru was the king of what province?

6. In what college is the Book of Kells on display today?

7. How did Vikings preserve their fish for the colder months? a) freezing b) pickling c) smoking

8. On what type of castle would you find ramparts, a barbican and a portcullis?

9. Granuaile sailed to England to ask Queen _____ to release her sons from captivity.

10. What were followers of King James II called?

Quiz

6

Round 1

1. What famous saint did King Niall of the Nine Hostages capture as a slave in Wales?

2. What was the name of the boats used by the Vikings?

3. What English king invaded Ireland in 1394 to try to gain control of the country? King R____ II.

4. The English army who fought at the Pass of the Plumes had what on their helmets? a) feathers b) wool c) leather

5. Was King James II Catholic or Protestant?

6. The ruling class of wealthy landowners in the 18th century was called the A_____.

7. Viscount Powerscourt's home in Dublin is now: a) a museum b) a restaurant c) a shopping centre.

8. True or false: Daniel O'Connell's meetings sometimes had up to 100,000 people in attendance.

9. The word 'Fenian' was inspired by the mythical soldiers of what legendary Irish warrior?

10. What did the *Titanic* collide with that caused it to sink?

Round 2

1. Which 1916 Rising leader married his fiancée in Kilmainham Gaol just seven hours before his execution? a) Seán Mac Diarmada b) James Connolly c) Joseph Mary Plunkett

2. Name the Irish painter who liked to paint landscapes and horses. Hint: His brother was a famous poet.

3. True or false: Two Irish women, Mairead Maguire and Betty Williams, won the Nobel Peace Prize in 1976 for promoting peace in Northern Ireland.

4. Name the Irish gatherings where people were entertained by poems and stories as well as music and dancing.

5. Sir Hans Sloane from Co. Down invented: a) hot chocolate b) chocolate spread c) chocolate milk.

6. Which of these languages would **NOT** have been taught in Irish hedge schools? a) English b) Greek c) French?

7. Which Irish president began to work for the United Nations after she finished her term?

8. Gastropods are fossils of what slimy, shelled creature?

9. Which is oldest: Newgrange, the pyramids in Egypt or Stonehenge in England?

10. What was the name of the Celtic goddess of summer and wealth? a) Aisling b) Áine c) Aoife

Round 3

1. A solar was a room in a Norman castle used as:
   a) a day room b) a dining room c) a bathroom.

2. *Ard Rí* means High ____ in English.

3. How old was St Patrick when he was captured as a
   slave? a) 16 b) 24 c) 10

4. A blunderbuss is a type of: a) hammer b) gun
   c) sword.

5. What town in Co. Louth did Oliver Cromwell
   attack first? D____.

6. True or false: The United Irishmen only had
   Catholic members.

7. Eileen Gray was an architect and furniture
   designer best known for her *Bibendum* a) coffee
   table b) chair c) wardrobe.

8. What famous French military leader promised
   Robert Emmet help in future revolutions?
   N____.

9. The poorest of people who were evicted by
   their landlords during the Famine were sent to
   w____.

10. What does 'GAA' stand for?

Round 4

1. How many lifeboats were on board the *Titanic*?
   a) 20 b) 35 c) 50

2. The British Government sent two new police forces to Ireland during the War of Independence: the Auxiliary Division and the B___ and T____.

3. Name the Nobel Prize-winning playwright from Dublin who wrote plays such as *Arms and the Man* and *Pygmalion*. George B_____ S_____.

4. Which of these nationalities were **NOT** Jacobites in the Battle of the Boyne? a) Irish b) Dutch c) French

5. The Vikings and the Irish kings fought each other at the Battle of C_____.

6. True or false: Married women in 13th-century Ireland would cover their heads with a hat.

7. What political party was founded by Éamon de Valera in 1926?

8. What was first added to film in 1927? a) sound b) colour c) special effects

9. What is another name for the 'New' Stone Age period? N_____.

10. The entry point for immigrants coming to America was ___ Island.

Round 5

1. Name the Irish Nationalist who was known as 'the Uncrowned King of Ireland'? C___ S___ P_____.

2. In order for women to vote in 1918, they had to be: a) over 18 b) over 21 c) over 30.

3. How many players are there on hurling and Gaelic football teams?

4. What illness caused Seán Mac Diarmada, one of the leaders of the 1916 Rising, to walk with a cane? a) leprosy b) polio c) arthritis

5. Ireland's most successful traditional music group is The C_____s.

6. The first greyhound track in Ireland was opened in what city in Ulster?

7. True or false: Soap operas are so called because soap detergents used to advertise on them.

8. In 1902 Ireland held its first: a) horse race b) greyhound race c) motorcycle race.

9. On 21 November 1920, known as Bloody Sunday, the British forces launched an attack in what sporting venue?

10. How many times has Ireland won the Eurovision song contest? a) two b) five c) seven

Quiz

7

Round 1

1. What currency was introduced to Ireland in 1999?

2. Queen Elizabeth I gave land to Sir Walter Raleigh in what Munster county?

3. Theobald Wolfe Tone died: a) in battle b) in prison c) in his home.

4. The flag of the United Irishmen was usually what colour?

5. Sir James Galway is one of the world's greatest players of what instrument: a) guitar b) flute c) violin.

6. Charles Stewart Parnell's sisters, Frances and Anna, set up the _____ Land League in 1881.

7. Which national sport is missing from this list of GAA sports: Gaelic football, handball, hurling and camogie?

8. What famous Irish Nationalist was nicknamed 'The Big Fellow'? Michael _____.

9. Normandy, named after the Normans, is a region of what country?

10. In the Irish myth, what did Cúchulainn use to kill Culann's hound?

Round 2

1. Name the witty Dublin writer known for plays such as *The Importance of Being Earnest* and his novel *The Picture of Dorian Gray*.

2. Which of these is **NOT** a suggested use for the Newgrange passage tomb? a) to worship the sun b) to predict the seasons c) to hide from invaders

3. Thatched roofs are made from: a) slate b) straw c) wood.

4. What was the very first metal to be discovered? a) silver b) bronze c) copper

5. The victory of the Battle of the B____ is celebrated on 12 July by Orange Order Protestants.

6. How many Irishmen died in World War I? a) 38,000 b) 49,000 c) 56,000

7. In what year did the Easter Rising take place?

8. From 1799 until 1851, a tax was put on houses with more than six: a) doors b) rooms c) windows.

9. What farm animal did Queen Maeve steal from Cúchulainn?

10. On Bloody Sunday, Tipperary was playing against what Leinster county in a Gaelic football match?

Round 3

1. Who came to Ireland first, the Vikings or the Normans?

2. Grace O'Malley wasn't allowed on voyages with her father because: a) her skirts were too wide b) her hair was too long c) her arms were too weak.

3. Which king passed the Penal Laws in Ireland? King W_____ of O_____.

4. Daniel Maclise was an artist in the 19th century who painted historical events such as the marriage of Strongbow and: a) Anna b) Ava c) Aoife.

5. In which Ulster county did St Patrick build a church, making it the Christian centre of Ireland?

6. True or false: The United Irish Army defeated the British at the Battle of Vinegar Hill.

7. Who said the following: 'Until my country has taken her place among the nations of the earth, then and not till then, let my epitaph be written'? Robert E____.

8. In 1926 Ireland launched its first: a) television station b) printing press c) radio station.

9. What type of megalithic tomb has at least one inner chamber that is reached through a long tunnel built of stone? P_____ tomb.

10. In what year did Ireland become a republic? a) 1916 b) 1938 c) 1949

Round 4

1. What Irish political party was founded in 1926?
    a) Fianna Fáil b) Fine Gael c) Sinn Féin

2. A tonsure is: a) a monk's robe b) a monk's sandals
    c) a monk's hairstyle.

3. True or false: Mary McAleese was the world's first
    female president to succeed another female.

4. Whose slogan was 'the land of Ireland for the
    people of Ireland'? Michael D____.

5. 'Weisfjord' is the Norse name for which town?

6. In a monastery, what was a lavabo? a) a reading
    room b) a dining room c) a washing room

7. Name the dreadful buildings where families
    lived in one-room flats made from abandoned
    Georgian townhouses? T_____.

8. What Nobel Prize-winning writer wrote the play
    Waiting for Godot? Samuel _____.

9. What shocking event caused High King Conchobar
    mac Nessa to lose his temper, making the ball
    lodged in his forehead pop out?

10. Who started writing her famous diary in 1942?

Round 5

1. Where did King James II flee to after he lost support in England? a) Germany b) France c) Spain

2. True or false: Sean-nós dancing is a group activity.

3. Spell 'Clonmacnoise'.

4. A battle was fought for two days by rebels at Ballynahinch in what Ulster county?

5. Some young Irish rebels cut their hair short to show support for the revolutionaries in France and were known as Croppies or C___ B___.

6. What was the name of the mound of earth that Norman castles were built on?

7. Michael Coleman was a musician known for playing: a) the harp b) the uilleann pipes c) the fiddle.

8. What were films called once sound was added to them?

9. What deathly disease arrived in Ireland in 1348?

10. Where Dáil Éireann sits today was once the home of the Duke of L_____.

Quiz

8

Round 1

1. What country did Robert Emmet flee to in order to avoid being captured? a) Germany b) France c) Italy

2. True or false: A Native American tribe donated money to the Irish during the Great Famine.

3. What does 'GPO' stand for?

4. The first episode of *The Late Late Show* was presented by G___ B___ in 1962.

5. Éamon de Valera served as Taoiseach for: a) 14 years b) 21 years c) 30 years.

6. Sir Walter Raleigh introduced what popular crop to Ireland?

7. Which of these places was **NOT** captured by Cromwell when he first arrived in Ireland: Wexford, Kilkenny, Cork or Carlow?

8. The American Revolutionary War was fought between 13 states in North America and G_____ B_____.

9. In 1845 what fraction of potatoes in Ireland were destroyed? a) one-fifth b) one-third c) one-half

10. Seán O'Casey is known for writing plays such as *Juno and the Paycock* and *The Plough and the* ____?

Round 2

1. In some early Irish cinemas, if you didn't have money you could pay with an empty: a) flower pot b) jam jar c) butter dish.

2. Structures known as promontory forts could be found in the _____ Age.

3. Patrick Sarsfield led the Irish Army to retreat to what city in Munster after the Battle of the Boyne?

4. A mantilla was used by Catholic women to: a) cover their shoulders b) cover their heads c) cover their faces.

5. What is the Irish name of the mythological land of eternal youth where Oisín lived?

6. What two languages did the Normans speak when they invaded Ireland?

7. The Battle of K_____ marked the end of the Nine Years' War.

8. Under the Penal Laws, Catholics could not carry: a) weapons b) money c) umbrellas.

9. Theobald Wolfe Tone travelled to what European country to get soldiers for a rebellion?

10. In 1841 the population of Ireland was over: a) 3 million b) 5 million c) 8 million.

Round 3

1. True or false: More civilians were killed in the Easter Rising than British soldiers or Irish rebels.

2. Women's suffrage means giving women the right to: a) work b) vote c) protest.

3. Louis le Brocquy was an artist known for his portraits, such as his painting of playwright S____ B____.

4. Gay Byrne hosted *The Late Late Show* for: a) 15 years b) 28 years c) 37 years.

5. What type of modern shoe has its roots in Ireland? a) stilettos b) brogues c) flip-flops

6. In 2014 Michael D. Higgins paid the first official state visit by an Irish president to: a) Germany b) Canada c) the United Kingdom.

7. What were Neolithic houses **NOT** built with? a) oak planks b) wattle c) animal skins

8. What singer released his album *Thriller* in 1982?

9. What era took place between the years 2500 BC and 500 BC and is famous for introducing the first metal tools and weapons?

10. What is the name of the harmful fairies that cause destruction on farms and at sea and can take many animal forms?

Round 4

1. What language is the Book of Kells written in?

2. Viking means 'p____ raid' in the Old Norse language.

3. What was the Black Death carried by? a) fleas b) mice c) cockroaches

4. Name the cruel sport, outlawed by Oliver Cromwell, where a dog attacks a chained-up bear.

5. Lord Maguire, Lord O'Neill and Lord O'Donnell, who fought in the Nine Years' War, all had the same first name: a) Harry b) Hugh c) Hector.

6. Which of these nationalities were **NOT** Williamites in the Battle of the Boyne? a) English b) French c) Spanish

7. The United Irishmen wore normal clothes, sometimes decorated with: a) fur b) feathers c) ribbons.

8. What yellow crop did the British Government import from America to try to help during the Great Famine?

9. Over how many people were killed in the War of Independence? a) 850 b) 1,000 c) 1,400

10. What play by John Millington Synge caused riots during its opening run at the Abbey Theatre? *The P____ of the W____ World.*

Round 5

1. The first-ever broadcast on Irish television was a speech by which president?

2. What is the name of the early Irish alphabet that consisted of lines and dots carved on stone?

3. A type of long, loose breeches worn by rich men in the 19th century were called: a) plus-threes b) plus-fours c) plus-fives.

4. A 'vardo' is a type of: a) wagon b) ship c) train.

5. Spell 'leprechaun'.

6. Which World War began in 1939?

7. In what county can you see tracks from a tetrapod left in the mud?

8. What is the name of the naughty fairy children who sometimes get swapped with human babies?

9. Crop rotation was a farming method introduced by: a) the Normans b) the Celts c) the Vikings.

10. What Queen caused a famine in Munster because the people had started a rebellion?

Quiz

9

Round 1

1. A battle fought between the Lord of Fermanagh and the English was named after what food?
   a) cakes b) puddings c) biscuits

2. Name the Irish political leader who was known for hating violence: D___ O'C_____.

3. True or false: Eoghan Ruadh O'Neill went to Donegal in 1642 to help the British settlers.

4. What were Catholics forbidden from buying during the Penal Laws? a) horses b) land
   c) furniture

5. The 1798 rebellion was most successful in what county beginning with 'W'?

6. Michael Collins was born in what county?

7. The Troubles lasted for: a) 10 years b) 20 years
   c) 30 years.

8. The first version of what famous British flag was designed in 1606?

9. Who set up the Church of England when the Pope would not end his first marriage? King ___
   VIII.

10. Who led the Norman army that landed in 1170?
    S___.

Round 2

1. In Celtic clothing, a léine was: a) a tunic b) a skirt c) a crown.

2. In what Ulster county were two of Ireland's biggest dinosaur discoveries made?

3. William Thompson invented the Kelvin scale, which measures: a) temperature b) liquid c) speed.

4. Which American president was assassinated in 1963?

5. What was the first university in Ireland to allow female students? a) University College Dublin b) National University of Ireland, Galway c) University College Cork

6. What animal feed made from dried grass did the Normans introduce?

7. A halberd is a type of: a) weapon b) fossil c) armour.

8. The Battle of the Boyne was fought between J_____ II and W_____ of Orange.

9. Wolfe Tone's grave is in what Leinster county?

10. A dord is a musical horn, which is the Irish version of what Australian instrument?

Round 3

1. True or false: The cottiers and spailpíns were the wealthiest people during the Great Famine.

2. RTÉ's first colour broadcast was the _____ ____ Contest.

3. C. S. Lewis is best known for writing *The Chronicles of Narnia*, a series of seven books, including *The ____, the ____ and the _____*.

4. William Orpen was an artist who painted pictures of scenes from what war?

5. Major Walter Gordon Wilson invented the first: a) army tank b) machine gun c) grenade.

6. What type of megalithic tombs have a giant capstone balanced on at least two entrance stones?

7. What was the only utensil used for cooking in Celtic times?

8. The cure for what disease was found in 1954? a) leprosy b) smallpox c) measles

9. The remains of what extinct elephant-like animal were found in Co. Waterford?

10. Balor was a Celtic giant who had: a) one big eye b) no nose c) four ears.

Round 4

1. What is the national emblem of Ireland?

2. What was the name of the stepmother in the legend *The Children of Lir*? a) Aoife b) Ava c) Aisling

3. Vellum, used to make the pages of the *Book of Kells*, is made from: a) sheepskin b) calfskin c) goatskin.

4. To what castle was Robert Emmet marching when his followers started a riot? D____ Castle.

5. Norman people were forbidden from doing which of these acts by the Statutes of Kilkenny? a) marrying an Irish person b) waving at an Irish person c) eating like an Irish person

6. The Battle of the Boyne was fought near what town in Co. Louth?

7. At which castle did Granuaile insist on staying and always having a place at the dinner table? a) Kilkenny Castle b) Howth Castle c) Slane Castle

8. Kitchens were set up during the Great Famine to feed what food to the poor?

9. True or false: Seamus Heaney won the Nobel Prize for Literature in 1995.

10. Harry Ferguson invented the modern version of what essential farming vehicle?

Round 5

1. 'Wykinglo' is the Norse name for which town?

2. What colour do leprechauns wear?

3. Who famously wouldn't move from her seat on a bus in 1955? Rosa _____.

4. The King of Leinster said St Brigid could have as much land as her what could cover? a) hair b) cloak c) dress

5. True or false: Ireland was once home to spotted hyenas.

6. In what year did the first person land on the moon? a) 1953 b) 1969 c) 1978

7. Some of the oldest fish traps in Europe were found near Spencer Dock in what county?

8. What is a St Brigid's Cross made from?

9. What was the name for a necklace made from twisted gold worn during the Bronze Age?

10. What country was Fionn mac Cumhaill trying to get to when he began building the Giant's Causeway?

Quiz

10

Round 1

1. What type of animal was sent to space for the first time in 1957? a) a dog b) a cat c) a monkey

2. What plant did St Patrick use to teach the Christian belief of three persons in one God?

3. The Céide Fields, an example of Neolithic farming, are found in what Connacht county?

4. There is a large statue of which nationalist leader at the bottom of O'Connell Street in Dublin?

5. In Celtic clothing, what was a crios? a) a shirt b) a belt c) shoes

6. Brian Boru was killed at the Battle of C____.

7. Aengus was the god of a) war b) love c) time.

8. True or false: High Crosses were used as grave markers.

9. In what Leinster county did the Normans land in 1169?

10. What was the name of the area that Henry VII took control of? The P___.

Round 2

1. Wolfe Tone tried to land at what bay with 14,000 French soldiers? a) Bantry Bay b) Clew Bay c) Donegal Bay

2. What county did English forces first attack in the Nine Years' War? a) Fermanagh b) Tyrone c) Donegal

3. Which of these was **NOT** one of the activities banned by Oliver Cromwell? a) going to the theatre b) drinking alcohol c) eating chocolate

4. William was the Prince of Orange in: a) Germany b) Holland c) France.

5. What type of writing did John Robert Gregg invent that was widely used by secretaries to take speedy notes?

6. Robert Emmet was arrested and imprisoned at K_____ Gaol in Dublin.

7. Daniel O'Connell's face was on the old a) £10 note b) £20 note c) £50 note.

8. The Society of St V____ de ____ was set up during the famine to distribute food to the poor.

9. The James Joyce novel *Ulysses* is set on 16 June 1904. This day is now known as what?

10. In ancient Ireland, communities held a festival called an *aonach*, usually at the same time as an important: a) funeral b) wedding c) birth.

Round 3

1. A flannel or cotton collarless shirt is often called: a) a mother shirt b) a grandad shirt c) a brother shirt.

2. In early national schools, children learned to write using: a) pen and paper b) parchment and quill c) slates and chalk.

3. Spell 'suffragettes'.

4. What Irish television channel was founded in 1961?

5. You can visit the *Dunbrody* famine ship in New Ross, Co. _____.

6. What type of megalithic tomb has a courtyard in front of the main entrance?

7. A gorget is a type of: a) clothing b) jewellery c) armour.

8. What province is named after King Conn Céadchathach?

9. What was the colour of the bull that Queen Maeve stole from Cúchulainn?

10. What date is St Patrick's Day?

Round 4

1. Leading up to the 1798 Rebellion, what province was the one area of Ireland where Catholics and Protestants had joined together?

2. What is another name for the Christian group the Society of Friends?

3. Daniel O'Connell was nicknamed 'The L_____' because he achieved Catholic emancipation.

4. What was the name of Fionn mac Cumhaill's teacher, who caught the Salmon of Knowledge? a) Fergal b) Finnegas c) Fintan

5. Which of the following is **NOT** a deadly disease from the time of the Great Famine? a) typhus b) cholera c) cooties

6. The first cinema in Ireland was established by the writer J___ J____.

7. The Beaufort Scale, invented by Francis Beaufort, measures: a) earthquakes b) wind c) rain.

8. Ghillies are a type of: a) dancing shoe b) work trousers c) reading glasses.

9. What red-haired puppet was born in 1979?

10. Who became the Queen of England in 1952 and is the longest-reigning monarch in British history?

Round 5

1. King Conn Céadchathach is said to have fought how many battles? a) one hundred b) one thousand c) one million

2. What song competition did Ireland enter for the first time in 1965?

3. Who was the first female president of Ireland?

4. What type of free school was introduced in 1967? a) free primary school b) free secondary school c) free third-level college

5. Name the conflict between Unionists and Nationalists in Northern Ireland that lasted from 1968–1998.

6. What province led a rebellion against Queen Elizabeth in 1580?

7. King Cormac mac Airt died when he choked on the bone of what type of fish?

8. What were the earliest Norman castles made from?

9. What Leinster county was formerly named King's County by Queen Mary I?

10. Wexford was declared a republic in 1798, which lasted for: a) three days b) three weeks c) three months.

ANSWERS

Quiz

1

Round 1

1. What stringed instrument is Brian Boru thought to have played?
   Harp

2. What was the most secure part of a Norman castle? a) the keep b) the tower c) the ramparts
   a) The keep

3. Which of these was **NOT** one of the Penal Laws?
   a) Catholics and Protestants couldn't marry
   b) Catholics could not become hairdressers
   c) Catholics couldn't adopt orphans
   b) Catholics could not become hairdressers

4. The building where monks spent their time writing and decorating holy books was called a s_____.
   Scriptorium

5. Which army won the Battle of the Boyne: the Williamites or the Jacobites?
   The Williamites

6. Crinoids are marine animals related to what five-pointed sea creature?
   Starfish

7. What did Fionn mac Cumhaill's wife dress him as to fool the giant Benandonner? a) a dog b) a baby c) a teddy bear
   b) a baby

8. The G____ L____ was formed in 1893 to promote spoken Irish.
   The Gaelic League

9. What type of houses were also called 'back-to-backs'? ____ houses.
   Terraced houses

10. True or false: In the 19th century, boys commonly wore dresses until they were six or seven.
    True

Round 2

1. The coracle was one of the first types of what in Europe? a) bicycle b) boat c) car
   b) boat

2. The war fought between Irish chieftains and the English Army during the Elizabethan era was known as the _____ Years' War.
   Nine Years' War

3. True or false: The King of Leinster invited the Vikings to Ireland to help him get his kingdom back.
   False – he invited the Normans

4. Ancient Irish warriors preserved what body part of their enemies so that they could show them off?
   Brains

5. What did the Mesolithic people **NOT** use to cover their tent-like shelters? a) thatch b) canvas c) animal hides.
   b) canvas

6. Famine ships were also known as _____ ships, because so many people died on board.
   Coffin ships

7. What Munster county beat Louth in the first Gaelic football All-Ireland final?
   Limerick

8. On what day of the week did the Easter Rising take place?
    Monday

9. Henry VIII ordered the closing of what across Ireland? a) schools b) hospitals c) monasteries?
    c) monasteries

10. Which poet and academic became the president of Ireland in 2011?
    Michael D. Higgins

Round 3

1. What is the name of the crescent-shaped collar made from thin sheets of gold worn during the Bronze Age? L____.
   Lunula

2. What first went on sale in 1944? a) staplers b) permanent markers c) ballpoint pens.
   c) ballpoint pens

3. What sweet, sticky food was used to flavour meat dishes in the Celtic era?
   Honey

4. Jerome O'Connor carved a statue of what famous Irish nationalist? Robert ____.
   Robert Emmet

5. True or false: Countess Markievicz was sentenced to death for participating in the 1916 rising.
   True – she was later pardoned

6. The Harland & Wolff shipyard where the *Titanic* was built is in which Irish city?
   Belfast

7. What is the name of the fungus that destroyed potato crops during the Great Famine? B____.
   Blight

8. What stringed instrument was on the United Irishmen's flag?
   Harp

9. How many Irish people were deported as slaves during Cromwell's conquest of Ireland?
   a) 10,000 b) 25,000 c) 50,000
   c) 50,000

10. Who was the UK's first female Prime Minister? Margaret _____.
   Margaret Thatcher

Round 4

1. What type of animal was a Scelidosaurus?
   Dinosaur

2. Which of these shapes is **NOT** carved into the decorated stones at Newgrange, Knowth and Dowth? a) spirals b) zig-zags c) hexagons
   c) hexagons

3. A new version of what flag was made when Ireland joined the United Kingdom?
   The Union Jack

4. Daniel O'Connell is buried in G____ Cemetery in Dublin.
   Glasnevin Cemetery

5. Jane Wilde, who was a writer for *The Nation* newspaper, was the mother of what famous writer?
   Oscar Wilde

6. James Connolly was born in: a) Scotland b) France c) Italy.
   a) Scotland

7. Bram Stoker was the author of what world-famous book about a spooky vampire?
   Dracula

8. Sir James Murray from Derry invented what medicine to relieve the Lord Lieutenant of Ireland of stomach pain?
   Milk of Magnesia

9. What was Cúchulainn's name before he defeated Culann's hound? S____.
   Setanta

10. Approximately how many people worldwide were killed by the Black Death? a) 10 million b) 45 million c) 75 million
    c) 75 million

Round 5

1. The Ascendancy were the only people in Ireland who had the right to: a) farm land b) vote c) marry.
   b) vote

2. What college in Dublin did Robert Emmet attend?
   Trinity College

3. Spell 'scriptorium'.
   Scriptorium

4. What war ended in 1975? The V_____ War.
   The Vietnam War

5. Palladius was sent by the Pope in 431 to be Ireland's first b___.
   Bishop

6. Granuaile was the P_____ Queen of Mayo.
   Pirate

7. 'Vadrefjord' is the Norse name for which county?
   Waterford

8. When is St Brigid's Day?
   1 February

9. In what decade was colour TV brought to Ireland?
   1970s

10. Was William of Orange Catholic or Protestant?
    Protestant

Quiz

2

Round 1

1. John Lavery was a painter known for painting the symbol of Éire, which was used on: a) Irish postage stamps b) Irish coins c) Irish banknotes.
   c) Irish banknotes

2. True or false: The Penal Laws were enforced for nearly 100 years.
   True

3. The biggest defeat of English forces in Irish history is known as the Battle of the _____ Ford. Hint: It's a colour!
   Yellow

4. Who became 'more Irish than the Irish themselves'? The N_____.
   The Normans

5. There was a shortage of what knitting material because of the Black Death?
   Wool

6. What type of bird were the Children of Lir turned into, according to legend?
   Swans

7. What is the most famous passage tomb in Ireland, found in Co. Meath?
   Newgrange

8. Fenians were members of the Fenian Brotherhood and the I____ R_____ B_____.
   Irish Republican Brotherhood

9. Name the Irish circus company that started in 1888 and is one of the oldest continuously touring circuses in the world. F_____ Circus.
   Fossett's Circus

10. In what county was the GAA founded?
    Tipperary

Round 2

1. Stirabout is a type of: a) hot drink b) watery porridge c) lumpy soup.
   c) lumpy soup

2. The United Irishmen wanted to break Ireland's connection with what country?
   England

3. True or false: Éamon de Valera was both the Taoiseach and President of Ireland in his lifetime.
   True

4. Those who did not support the 1921 treaty were called the _____.
   Irregulars

5. How did Daniel O'Connell arrive at his meetings? a) on horseback b) on a bicycle c) in a carriage.
   c) in a carriage

6. Y____ Ireland was a movement that involved Catholics and Protestants who wanted to bring about equality and wanted Ireland to have its own parliament.
   Young Ireland

7. How were the rooms inside a Norman castle lit?
   By candles

8. In 1642 the Irish leaders decided that the Irish people had to obey the laws of King C___.
   King Charles

9. Anne Devlin, known for her bravery in the 1803 revolution, was Robert Emmet's: a) sister b) girlfriend c) housekeeper.
   c) housekeeper

10. In 1918, what group of people was given the right to vote in Ireland?
    Women

Round 3

1. Sir Edward Carson was the leader of the Ulster
   V_____ F___.
   Ulster Volunteer Force

2. What is the name of the mythological fairy
   woman who cries when someone dies?
   Banshee

3. What hill in Co. Meath is believed to have been
   the seat of the high king in Ireland?
   Hill of Tara

4. What was the name of the strong honey drink
   favoured by the Vikings?
   Mead

5. When a landowner in Co. Mayo was ignored and
   excluded by his community for refusing to reduce
   rents, what new word was introduced to the
   English language? B_____.
   Boycott

6. Who wrote the novels *Ulysses* and *A Portrait of
   the Artist as a Young Man*? J___ J____.
   James Joyce

7. What Munster county did the Normans land in
   during their second invasion of 1170?
   Waterford

THE HISTOROPEDIA QUIZ BOOK

8. From what fish did Fionn mac Cumhaill gain his knowledge?
   Salmon

9. True or false: Daniel O'Connell did not support Robert Emmet's revolution of 1803.
   True

10. What Irish show is the world's second-longest running talk show?
    The Late Late Show

Round 4

1. Who began to settle in Ireland during the Iron Age? The C___.
   The Celts

2. The Battle of the B___ took place in 1690.
   Battle of the Boyne

3. What did people call the illegal radio stations that appeared with the invention of radio? Hint: Shiver me timbers!
   Pirate radio

4. Hitting or slapping children in schools was made illegal in Ireland in: a) 1964 b) 1979 c) 1982.
   c) 1982

5. In what county beginning with 'C' would you find Brownshill Dolmen, which has the largest capstone in Europe?
   Co. Carlow

6. True or false: The Irish chieftains defeated the English at the Battle of Kinsale.
   False – the Irish were defeated

7. Which of the following was **NOT** on board the *Titanic*? a) a gym b) a basketball court c) dog kennels
   b) a basketball court

8. John Philip Holland from Co. Clare is known for inventing the: a) hot air balloon b) kayak c) submarine.
c) submarine

9. What was the name of the small buildings that monks slept in?
Cells

10. Who arrived in Ireland in 1649 as the Lord Protector of Ireland to get revenge for how British settlers were treated? O_____ C_____.
Oliver Cromwell

Round 5

1. The Irish Parliament called for volunteer soldiers to protect the country while the rest of the British troops were sent to fight in: a) North America b) South Africa c) Eastern Asia.
   a) North America

2. True or false: Almost 400,000 people emigrated during the Great Famine.
   False – it was approximately one million

3. What was the name for the groups of huts built on stilts or man-made islands in a lake? C____.
   Crannógs

4. A Mesolithic campsite with animal bones was found at Mount Sandel in which Ulster county?
   Co. Derry

5. On which mountains in Antrim did St Patrick mind sheep? S____ Mountains.
   Slemish Mountains

6. What was the flowery name of the civil war between York and Lancaster in 1455? War of the ____.
   War of the Roses

7. The decisive battle of the 1798 rebellion was fought at: a) Ketchup Hill b) Vinegar Hill c) Salty Hill.
   b) Vinegar Hill

8. Daniel O'Connell organised _____ meetings. Hint: They weren't as scary as they sound!
   Monster meetings

9. What poet, remembered as Ireland's 'national poet', wrote 'Down by the Salley Gardens' and 'The Lake Isle of Innisfree'? William ____ ____.
   William Butler Yeats

10. What was the type of armour worn by the Normans? C___ ___.
    Chain mail

Quiz

3

Round 1

1. Which came first, the sinking of the *Titanic* or the Great Famine?
    The Great Famine

2. What is the name of the enclosure surrounding the motte of a Norman castle?
    Bailey

3. What civil rights leader and activist was assassinated in 1968? Martin L___ K___ Jr.
    Martin Luther King Jr

4. What language did Granuaile and the Queen have to speak when they met? a) English b) Irish c) Latin
    c) Latin

5. Daniel O'Connell founded the C___ Association, dedicated to bringing religious freedom to Ireland.
    Catholic Association

6. True or false: Third-class passengers on the *Titanic* were those closest to the lifeboats.
    False – the first-class passengers were closest to the lifeboats

7. In the Stone Age, people lived in huts built of w___ and d___.
    Wattle and daub

8. A cesspit was a Viking: a) bath b) toilet c) bed.
   b) toilet

9. Who was the father of Oisín, who lived in Tír na
   nÓg?
   Fionn mac Cumhaill

10. Complete the famous phrase by Theobald Wolfe
    Tone: 'Many suffer so that someday all Irish
    people may know j____ and p____.'
    Justice and peace

Round 2

1. The famous GAA venue on Jones' Road in Dublin was named after Archbishop Thomas ____.
   Thomas Croke

2. The walls built to separate Catholic and Protestant communities in towns in Northern Ireland are called ____ Lines.
   Peace Lines

3. You can visit a mass grave from the Great Famine in the town of Skibbereen in what county?
   Co. Cork

4. Who did Cromwell send to take his place in Ireland when he returned to England? a) his brother b) his second cousin c) his son-in-law
   c) his son-in-law

5. Who lived with Oisín in Tír na nÓg? a) Niamh b) Nora c) Nessa
   a) Niamh

6. In the 13th century, Irish men were noted for wearing ____ without a beard.
   Moustaches

7. What 1916 Rising leader was a poet who established two schools which were dedicated to teaching children through Irish? P____ P____.
   Pádraig Pearse

8. What type of rock is used to decorate the wall in front of Newgrange? a) quartz b) marble c) basalt?
   a) quartz

9. In Irish, which month is named after Lug, the god of harvest and light?
   August

10. The Republic of Connacht, established in 1798, lasted for: a) 12 days b) 12 weeks c) 12 months.
    a) 12 days

Round 3

1. The remains of what now-extinct animal can be found in Dublin's National History Museum? Irish e__.
    Irish elk

2. Granuaile (Gráinne Mhaol) means: a) bald Gráinne b) tall Gráinne c) ugly Gráinne.
    a) bald Gráinne

3. True or false: Protestant workers, farmers and shopkeepers were considered part of the Ascendancy.
    False – it was mainly just the upper class

4. When William Gladstone's Home Rule Bill was defeated it caused serious riots in what Irish city?
    Belfast

5. What is the name for a storyteller in Irish?
    Seanchaí

6. Thomas MacDonagh commanded the Volunteers in J_____ biscuit factory during the 1916 Rising.
    Jacob's

7. What metal is made when tin is added to copper?
    Bronze

8. What material was invented in 1907? a) cotton b) plastic c) rubber.
    b) plastic

9. True or false: Early Irish national schools had chairs with no backs on them.
   True

10. The G____ F____ Agreement was signed in 1998 and signalled an end to the Troubles in Northern Ireland.
    Good Friday Agreement

Round 4

1. Brian Boru is buried in what county in Ulster?
    Co. Armagh

2. A St Brigid's Cross is said to protect your home from what?
    Fire

3. Which of these is **NOT** a symptom of the bubonic plague? a) black boils b) vomiting blood c) hair loss
    c) hair loss

4. In which province was there a rebellion against English and Scottish settlers in 1641?
    Ulster

5. What metal was worn by the rich and powerful during the Bronze Age and was used to make ornaments and jewellery?
    Gold

6. What college in Dublin was established in 1592?
    Trinity College

7. Daniel O'Connell moved to France to study: a) medicine b) law c) education.
    b) law

8. Seven Young Irelanders were taken to Van Diemen's Land, now part of Australia and known as T_____.
    Tasmania

9. How many leaders of the Easter Rising were executed? a) 10 b) 16 c) 22
   b) 16

10. The *Book of Kells* and the *Book of Armagh* are examples of i_____ manuscripts.
    Illuminated

Round 5

1. Dr Francis Rynd from Dublin invented a type of:
   a) plaster b) syringe c) thermometer.
   b) syringe

2. True or false: The first bicycle was invented in Germany and had no pedals.
   True

3. Which came first, the Battle of the Boyne or the Nine Years' War?
   Nine Years' War

4. An Ichthyosaur was a large marine reptile, resembling what modern-day water mammal?
   Dolphin

5. In the myth, Aengus fell in love with a woman called Caer, who turned into what bird every two years?
   Swan

6. What Scandinavian country did the Vikings who raided Ireland come from?
   Norway

7. Which king started the Tudor period in England? King _____ VII.
   King Henry VII

8. Oliver Cromwell wanted to have his portrait painted with '_____ and all'.
   Warts

9. If a Catholic became a Protestant during the time of the Penal Laws, they were allowed to take:
   a) their neighbour's house b) their parents' land
   c) their brother's livestock.
   b) their parents' land

10. A selkie is an Irish mythological creature that appears as what marine animal during the day?
    Brown seal

Quiz

4

Round 1

1. The United Irishmen were a group inspired by the American and F____ Revolutions.
   French

2. Was Daniel O'Connell Catholic or Protestant?
   Catholic

3. In what year was the World Wide Web invented?
   a) 1989 b) 1995 c) 1971
   a) 1989

4. Every child in school once had a tally stick which recorded the amount of times they: a) talked in class b) got a question wrong c) spoke in Irish.
   c) spoke in Irish

5. What political party was founded in 1905 by Arthur Griffith? S___ F___.
   Sinn Féin

6. John H____ and David T____ were awarded the Nobel Peace Prize in 1998 for their work in ending the Troubles in Northern Ireland.
   John Hume and David Trimble

7. It's believed that the traditional Irish harp may have come from: a) Spain b) Turkey c) Egypt.
   c) Egypt

8. Lilting, used instead of instruments to provide a beat for dancers, is also called '____ music'.
   Mouth music

9. True or false: According to medieval Brehon Law, slaves could wear cloaks with only two colours.
   False – they could only wear one colour

10. High King Labraid Loingsech wanted to hide the fact that he had what type of ears?
    Horse's ears

Round 2

1. 1900 marked the death of which Irish playwright and novelist? Oscar _____.
   Oscar Wilde

2. Around what year did the first people come to Ireland? a) 6000 BC b) 8000 BC c) 4000 BC
   b) 8000 BC

3. Name the hole in the ground filled with water that could have been used for cooking meat or bathing during the Bronze Age.
   Fulacht fiadh

4. What reptile is St Patrick said to have driven out of Ireland?
   Snakes

5. True or false: The lords and ladies slept in the upper portion of a Norman castle.
   True

6. Grace O'Malley, the most feared pirate in Ireland, was better known by what name?
   Granuaile

7. The few survivors of Cromwell's first attack were sent where to work as slaves? a) Barbados b) Jamaica c) The Bahamas
   a) Barbados

8. During the time of the Penal Laws, some Catholics sent their children to ___ schools, where children were taught in secret.
   Hedge schools

9. Rebel leaders from the 1798 Rebellion had their heads cut off and stuck on spikes in what town? W____.
   Wexford

10. How much did the Catholic Association collect per month from its supporters? a) one penny b) sixpence c) one pound
    a) one penny

Round 3

1. You can visit a famine ship in Dublin called the
   J____ J_____.
   Jeanie Johnston

2. What did Michael Davitt found in 1879, which
   organised protests against unfair rents, taxes and
   evictions?
   The Land League

3. Tipperary beat what Connacht county in the first
   hurling All-Ireland final?
   Co. Galway

4. What is the name of the Parliament of Ireland?
   Dáil Éireann

5. In what year was a ceasefire called between
   Loyalists and Nationalists in Northern Ireland?
   a) 1981 b) 1997 c) 2000
   b) 1997

6. The C____ Brothers were an influential Irish folk
   group popular in the 1960s.
   The Clancy Brothers

7. Name the games played in Ireland that are almost
   as old as the Olympic Games.
   Tailteann Games

8. Sir James Martin, born in Co. Down, invented:
   a) the ejector seat b) the telescope c) the cornflake.
   a) the ejector seat

9. What Irish airline was started in 1936?
   Aer Lingus

10. Spell 'Neolithic'.
    Neolithic

Round 4

1. What type of stone was mostly used by the
   Mesolithic people to make tools? a) basalt
   b) limestone c) flint
   c) flint

2. Badb was a Celtic goddess of war who was able to
   turn into what bird?
   Crow

3. Ireland is known as 'the land of saints and _____'?
   Scholars

4. True or false: The Normans originally came from
   Denmark, Norway and Iceland.
   True

5. What Leinster county was formerly named
   Queen's County by Queen Mary I?
   Co. Laois

6. Many earls had to go to Europe after the Battle
   of Kinsale. This was known as the ____ of the
   Earls.
   Flight of the Earls

7. The followers of William of Orange were called
   W_____.
   Williamites

8. During the time of the Penal Laws, the
    Volunteers were noted for their: a) unusual
    hairstyles b) colourful uniforms c) shiny boots.
    b) colourful uniforms

9. What province benefited the most from the Act
    of Union, as lots of jobs were created?
    Ulster

10. How long did Daniel O'Connell spend in prison?
    a) three days b) three months c) three years
    b) three months

Round 5

1. What crop did poor people depend on in the time of the Great Famine?
   Potatoes

2. True or false: The Fenian Brotherhood was set up in the United States.
   True

3. Pádraig Pearse famously said '*tír gan teanga, tír gan anam*', which means 'a country without a _____ is a country without a soul'.
   Language

4. In what year did the *Titanic* sink? a) 1905 b) 1912 c) 1921
   b) 1912

5. Who was the leader of the Irish Republican Army during the War of Independence?
   Michael Collins

6. George Bernard Shaw's play *Pygmalion* inspired the musical *My ___ Lady*.
   My Fair Lady

7. Follies are strange buildings because: a) they had no doors b) they had no roof c) they had no real purpose.
   c) they had no real purpose

8. What American president visited Ireland in 1963?
   J___ F. _____.
   John F. Kennedy

9. Name the type of knitted jumper that comes from Galway.
   Aran jumper

10. Who was Ireland's first president from Northern Ireland?
    Mary McAleese

Quiz

5

Round 1

1. Which came first, the Iron Age or the Bronze Age?
   The Bronze Age

2. What famous ship sank in 1912?
   Titanic

3. What type of megalithic tomb is Newgrange?
   Passage tomb

4. The Turoe Stone, an example of the La Tène style of art, was found in what Connacht county?
   Co. Galway

5. What statue, by sculptor John Henry Foley, is situated on O'Connell Street in Dublin?
   Daniel O'Connell

6. In what room would the lord and lady of a Norman castle host dinner and watch minstrels perform? Great ___.
   Great Hall

7. Caravels and galleys are types of: a) weapons b) boats c) shelters.
   b) boats

8. When Cromwell's son-in-law had captured most of Ireland, Irish Catholic landowners were told to go 'to Hell or to _____'.
   Connacht

9. True or false: Catholic bishops, priests, monks and nuns had to leave Ireland under the Penal Laws.
   True

10. Samuel Nielson and Lord Edward Fitzgerald planned a rising in what Irish city for 23 May 1798?
    Dublin

Round 2

1. When Ireland joined the United Kingdom, they were ruled by a parliament in which English city?
   London

2. Daniel O'Connell ran for an election held in what county?
   Co. Clare

3. Isaac Butt from Donegal started the H__ R__ League in 1873.
   Home Rule League

4. What GAA competition was first held in 1887?
   All-Ireland Championships

5. Whose widow was elected as a TD in the First and Second Dála? a) Pádraig Pearse b) Thomas MacDonagh c) Thomas J. Clarke
   c) Thomas J. Clarke

6. Countess _____ was heavily involved in the 1916 Rising and was one of the first women in the world to hold a cabinet position.
   Markievicz

7. Peig Sayers wrote her book *Peig* about life on which islands off Co. Kerry?
   Blasket Islands

8. Evie Hone and Harry Clarke are both artists that are known for: a) marble statues b) stained glass c) wooden carvings.
   b) stained glass

9. Thomas Smith from Dublin invented what cream used for nappy rash and other skin problems?
   Sudocrem

10. What common vegetable can be found in colcannon, boxty and champ?
    Potato

Round 3

1. What was the first canal built in Ireland?
    The Grand Canal

2. In what year did World War I begin? a) 1918
    b) 1912 c) 1914
    c) 1914

3. Was Megalosaurus a carnivore or a herbivore?
    Carnivore

4. On which day every year is the inner chamber of
    Newgrange illuminated at sunrise?
    Winter solstice

5. What is the Irish name for a kingdom?
    Tuath

6. Which of these was **NOT** one of the purposes of
    a round tower? a) to call people to church b) to
    sleep in c) to hide in times of danger
    b) to sleep in

7. Who introduced coinage to Ireland? a) the Celts
    b) the Vikings c) the Normans
    b) the Vikings

8. What was another name for the bubonic plague?
    The Black Death

9.   Soldiers from what European country came to
     help the Irish chieftains in the Battle of Kinsale?
       Spain

10. True or false: Oliver Cromwell made it against the
     law to celebrate Christmas.
       True

Round 4

1. What harsh new laws were introduced to Ireland in 1695?
    The Penal Laws

2. The leader of the United Irishmen was Theobald W___ T___.
    Wolfe Tone

3. Daniel O'Connell's final meeting was set to be held in: a) Clondalkin b) Clontarf c) Cork.
    b) Clontarf

4. In what Munster county was the Irish tricolour flag first raised?
    Co. Waterford

5. When did Conradh na Gaeilge succeed in introducing Irish into primary school classrooms? a) 1880 b) 1900 c) 1920
    b) 1900

6. Éamonn Ceannt, one of the leaders of the 1916 Rising, was a talented player of which Irish instrument?
    Uilleann pipes

7. True or false: Michael Collins did not support the 1921 treaty.
    False

8.   Jonathan Swift wrote what book about tiny people on the island of Lilliput? _____ *Travels*.
     Gulliver's Travels

9.   What type of horse racing was invented in Ireland in the 18th century? a) steeplechasing b) flat racing c) endurance racing
     a) steeplechasing

10. Traditional flat caps, or 'Paddy caps', are made of what woollen fabric?
     Tweed

Round 5

1. Who was the first president of Ireland?
   Douglas Hyde

2. Spell 'Newgrange'.
   Newgrange

3. Echinoids are a type of fossilised: a) sea horse
   b) sea urchin c) sea anemone.
   b) sea urchin

4. What is the name for the large circular mound of
   a passage tomb? C____.
   Cairn

5. Brian Boru was the king of what province?
   Munster

6. In what college is the Book of Kells on display
   today?
   Trinity College

7. How did Vikings preserve their fish for the colder
   months? a) freezing b) pickling c) smoking
   c) smoking

8. On what type of castle would you find ramparts, a
   barbican and a portcullis?
   Norman castle

9. Granuaile sailed to England to ask Queen
    _____ to release her sons from captivity.
    Elizabeth

10. What were followers of King James II called?
    Jacobites

Quiz

6

Round 1

1. What famous saint did King Niall of the Nine Hostages capture as a slave in Wales?
   St Patrick

2. What was the name of the boats used by the Vikings?
   Longboat

3. What English king invaded Ireland in 1394 to try to gain control of the country? King R___ II.
   King Richard II

4. The English army who fought at the Pass of the Plumes had what on their helmets? a) feathers b) wool c) leather
   a) feathers

5. Was King James II Catholic or Protestant?
   Catholic

6. The ruling class of wealthy landowners in the 18th century was called the A_____.
   Ascendancy

7. Viscount Powerscourt's home in Dublin is now: a) a museum b) a restaurant c) a shopping centre.
   c) a shopping centre

8. True or false: Daniel O'Connell's meetings sometimes had up to 100,000 people in attendance.
    True

9. The word 'Fenian' was inspired by the mythical soldiers of what legendary Irish warrior?
    Fionn mac Cumhaill

10. What did the *Titanic* collide with that caused it to sink?
    An iceberg

Round 2

1. Which 1916 Rising leader married his fiancée in Kilmainham Gaol just seven hours before his execution? a) Seán Mac Diarmada b) James Connolly c) Joseph Mary Plunkett
   c) Joseph Mary Plunkett

2. Name the Irish painter who liked to paint landscapes and horses. Hint: His brother was a famous poet.
   Jack B. Yeats

3. True or false: Two Irish women, Mairead Maguire and Betty Williams, won the Nobel Peace Prize in 1976 for promoting peace in Northern Ireland.
   True

4. Name the Irish gatherings where people were entertained by poems and stories as well as music and dancing.
   Céilí

5. Sir Hans Sloane from Co. Down invented: a) hot chocolate b) chocolate spread c) chocolate milk.
   c) chocolate milk

6. Which of these languages would **NOT** have been taught in Irish hedge schools? a) English b) Greek c) French?
   c) French

7. Which Irish president began to work for the
   United Nations after she finished her term?
   Mary Robinson

8. Gastropods are fossils of what slimy, shelled
   creature?
   Snails

9. Which is oldest: Newgrange, the pyramids in
   Egypt or Stonehenge in England?
   Newgrange

10. What was the name of the Celtic goddess of
    summer and wealth? a) Aisling b) Áine c) Aoife
    Áine

Round 3

1. A solar was a room in a Norman castle used as:
   a) a day room b) a dining room c) a bathroom.
   a) a day room

2. *Ard Rí* means High ___ in English.
   High King

3. How old was St Patrick when he was captured as a slave? a) 16 b) 24 c) 10
   a) 16

4. A blunderbuss is a type of: a) hammer b) gun c) sword.
   b) gun

5. What town in Co. Louth did Oliver Cromwell attack first? D_____.
   Drogheda

6. True or false: The United Irishmen only had Catholic members.
   False

7. Eileen Gray was an architect and furniture designer best known for her Bibendum a) coffee table b) chair c) wardrobe.
   b) chair

8. What famous French military leader promised
    Robert Emmet help in future revolutions?
    N_____.
    Napoleon

9. The poorest of people who were evicted by
    their landlords during the Famine were sent to
    w_____.
    workhouses

10. What does 'GAA' stand for?
    Gaelic Athletic Association

Round 4

1. How many lifeboats were on board the *Titanic*?
   a) 20 b) 35 c) 50
      a) 20

2. The British Government sent two new police
   forces to Ireland during the War of Independence:
   the Auxiliary Division and the B___ and T___.
      Black and Tans

3. Name the Nobel Prize-winning playwright from
   Dublin who wrote plays such as *Arms and the Man*
   and *Pygmalion*. George B____ S____.
      George Bernard Shaw

4. Which of these nationalities were **NOT** Jacobites
   in the Battle of the Boyne? a) Irish b) Dutch
   c) French
      b) Dutch

5. The Vikings and the Irish kings fought each other
   at the Battle of C____.
      Battle of Clontarf

6. True or false: Married women in 13th-century
   Ireland would cover their heads with a hat.
      True

7. What political party was founded by Éamon de
   Valera in 1926?
      Fianna Fáil

8. What was first added to film in 1927? a) sound
   b) colour c) special effects
   a) sound

9. What is another name for the 'New' Stone Age
   period? N_____.
   Neolithic

10. The entry point for immigrants coming to
    America was ___ Island.
    Ellis Island

Round 5

1. Name the Irish Nationalist who was known as 'the Uncrowned King of Ireland'? C___ S___ P____.
   Charles Stuart Parnell

2. In order for women to vote in 1918, they had to be: a) over 18 b) over 21 c) over 30.
   c) over 30

3. How many players are there on hurling and Gaelic football teams?
   15

4. What illness caused Seán Mac Diarmada, one of the leaders of the 1916 Rising, to walk with a cane? a) leprosy b) polio c) arthritis
   b) polio

5. Ireland's most successful traditional music group is The C_____s.
   The Chieftains

6. The first greyhound track in Ireland was opened in what city in Ulster?
   Belfast

7. True or false: Soap operas are so called because soap detergents used to advertise on them.
   True

8. In 1902 Ireland held its first: a) horse race
    b) greyhound race c) motorcycle race.
      c) motorcycle race

9. On 21 November 1920, known as Bloody Sunday,
    the British forces launched an attack in what
    sporting venue?
      Croke Park

10. How many times has Ireland won the Eurovision
    song contest? a) two b) five c) seven
      c) seven

Quiz

7

Round 1

1. What currency was introduced to Ireland in 1999?
   Euro

2. Queen Elizabeth I gave land to Sir Walter Raleigh in what Munster county?
   Co. Cork

3. Theobald Wolfe Tone died: a) in battle b) in prison c) in his home.
   b) in prison

4. The flag of the United Irishmen was usually what colour?
   Green

5. Sir James Galway is one of the world's greatest players of what instrument: a) guitar b) flute c) violin.
   b) flute

6. Charles Stewart Parnell's sisters, Frances and Anna, set up the _____ Land League in 1881.
   Ladies' Land League

7. Which national sport is missing from this list of GAA sports: Gaelic football, handball, hurling and camogie?
   Rounders

8. What famous Irish Nationalist was nicknamed
    'The Big Fellow'? Michael _____.
    Michael Collins

9. Normandy, named after the Normans, is a region
    of what country?
    France

10. In the Irish myth, what did Cúchulainn use to kill
    Culann's hound?
    A sliotar

Round 2

1. Name the witty Dublin writer known for plays
   such as *The Importance of Being Earnest* and his
   novel *The Picture of Dorian Gray*.
   Oscar Wilde

2. Which of these is **NOT** a suggested use for the
   Newgrange passage tomb? a) to worship the sun
   b) to predict the seasons c) to hide from invaders
   c) to hide from invaders

3. Thatched roofs are made from: a) slate b) straw
   c) wood.
   b) straw

4. What was the very first metal to be discovered?
   a) silver b) bronze c) copper
   c) copper

5. The victory of the Battle of the B____
   is celebrated on 12 July by Orange Order
   Protestants.
   Battle of the Boyne

6. How many Irishmen died in World War I?
   a) 38,000 b) 49,000 c) 56,000
   b) 49,000

7. In what year did the Easter Rising take place?
   1916

8. From 1799 until 1851, a tax was put on houses with more than six: a) doors b) rooms c) windows.
   c) windows

9. What farm animal did Queen Maeve steal from Cúchulainn?
   A bull

10. On Bloody Sunday, Tipperary was playing against what Leinster county in a Gaelic football match?
    Co. Dublin

Round 3

1. Who came to Ireland first, the Vikings or the Normans?
   The Vikings

2. Grace O'Malley wasn't allowed on voyages with her father because: a) her skirts were too wide b) her hair was too long c) her arms were too weak.
   b) her hair was too long

3. Which king passed the Penal Laws in Ireland? King W_____ of O_____.
   William of Orange

4. Daniel Maclise was an artist in the 19th century who painted historical events such as the marriage of Strongbow and: a) Anna b) Ava c) Aoife.
   c) Aoife

5. In which Ulster county did St Patrick build a church, making it the Christian centre of Ireland?
   Co. Armagh

6. True or false: The United Irish Army defeated the British at the Battle of Vinegar Hill.
   False

7. Who said the following: 'Until my country has taken her place among the nations of the earth, then and not till then, let my epitaph be written'? Robert E____.
   Robert Emmet

8. In 1926 Ireland launched its first: a) television
    station b) printing press c) radio station.
    c) radio station

9. What type of megalithic tomb has at least one
    inner chamber that is reached through a long
    tunnel built of stone? P_____ tomb.
    Passage tomb

10. In what year did Ireland become a republic?
    a) 1916 b) 1938 c) 1949
    c) 1949

Round 4

1. What Irish political party was founded in 1926?
   a) Fianna Fáil b) Fine Gael c) Sinn Féin
   Fianna Fáil

2. A tonsure is: a) a monk's robe b) a monk's sandals
   c) a monk's hairstyle.
   c) a monk's hairstyle

3. True or false: Mary McAleese was the world's first
   female president to succeed another female.
   True

4. Whose slogan was 'the land of Ireland for the
   people of Ireland'? Michael D____.
   Michael Davitt

5. 'Weisfjord' is the Norse name for which town?
   Wexford

6. In a monastery, what was a lavabo? a) a reading
   room b) a dining room c) a washing room
   c) a washing room

7. Name the dreadful buildings where families
   lived in one-room flats made from abandoned
   Georgian townhouses? T____.
   Tenements

8. What Nobel Prize-winning writer wrote the play
   Waiting for Godot? Samuel _____.
   Samuel Beckett

9. What shocking event caused High King Conchobar
    mac Nessa to lose his temper, making the ball
    lodged in his forehead pop out?
    The death of Jesus Christ

10. Who started writing her famous diary in 1942?
    Anne Frank

Round 5

1. Where did King James II flee to after he lost
   support in England? a) Germany b) France
   c) Spain
   b) France

2. True or false: Sean-nós dancing is a group activity.
   False – it's a solo dance

3. Spell 'Clonmacnoise'.
   Clonmacnoise

4. A battle was fought for two days by rebels at
   Ballynahinch in what Ulster county?
   Co. Down

5. Some young Irish rebels cut their hair short to
   show support for the revolutionaries in France
   and were known as Croppies or C____ B___.
   Croppy Boys

6. What was the name of the mound of earth that
   Norman castles were built on?
   Motte

7. Michael Coleman was a musician known for
   playing: a) the harp b) the uilleann pipes c) the
   fiddle.
   c) the fiddle

8. What were films called once sound was added to
    them?
    Talkies

9. What deathly disease arrived in Ireland in 1348?
    The Black Death

10. Where Dáil Éireann sits today was once the home
    of the Duke of L_____.
    Duke of Leinster

Quiz

8

Round 1

1. What country did Robert Emmet flee to in order
   to avoid being captured? a) Germany b) France
   c) Italy
   b) France

2. True or false: A Native American tribe donated
   money to the Irish during the Great Famine.
   True

3. What does 'GPO' stand for?
   General Post Office

4. The first episode of *The Late Late Show* was
   presented by G___ B___ in 1962.
   Gay Byrne

5. Éamon de Valera served as Taoiseach for:
   a) 14 years b) 21 years c) 30 years.
   b) 21 years

6. Sir Walter Raleigh introduced what popular crop
   to Ireland?
   Potatoes

7. Which of these places was **NOT** captured
   by Cromwell when he first arrived in Ireland:
   Wexford, Kilkenny, Cork or Carlow?
   Cork

THE HISTOROPEDIA QUIZ BOOK

8. The American Revolutionary War was fought between 13 states in North America and G_____ B_____.

   Great Britain

9. In 1845 what fraction of potatoes in Ireland were destroyed? a) one-fifth b) one-third c) one-half

   b) one-third

10. Seán O'Casey is known for writing plays such as *Juno and the Paycock* and *The Plough and the* ____?

    The Plough and the Stars

142

Round 2

1. In some early Irish cinemas, if you didn't have money you could pay with an empty: a) flower pot b) jam jar c) butter dish.
   b) jam jar

2. Structures known as promontory forts could be found in the _____ Age.
   Iron Age

3. Patrick Sarsfield led the Irish Army to retreat to what city in Munster after the Battle of the Boyne?
   Limerick

4. A mantilla was used by Catholic women to: a) cover their shoulders b) cover their heads c) cover their faces.
   b) cover their heads

5. What is the Irish name of the mythological land of eternal youth where Oisín lived?
   Tír na nÓg

6. What two languages did the Normans speak when they invaded Ireland?
   French and English

7. The Battle of K_____ marked the end of the Nine Years' War.
   Battle of Kinsale

8. Under the Penal Laws, Catholics could not carry:
    a) weapons b) money c) umbrellas.
    a) weapons

9. Theobald Wolfe Tone travelled to what European
    country to get soldiers for a rebellion?
    France

10. In 1841 the population of Ireland was over:
    a) 3 million b) 5 million c) 8 million.
    c) 8 million

Round 3

1. True or false: More civilians were killed in the Easter Rising than British soldiers or Irish rebels.
   True

2. Women's suffrage means giving women the right to: a) work b) vote c) protest.
   b) vote

3. Louis le Brocquy was an artist known for his portraits, such as his painting of playwright S____ B____.
   Samuel Beckett

4. Gay Byrne hosted *The Late Late Show* for: a) 15 years b) 28 years c) 37 years.
   c) 37 years

5. What type of modern shoe has its roots in Ireland? a) stilettos b) brogues c) flip-flops
   b) brogues

6. In 2014 Michael D. Higgins paid the first official state visit by an Irish president to: a) Germany b) Canada c) the United Kingdom.
   c) the United Kingdom

7. What were Neolithic houses **NOT** built with? a) oak planks b) wattle c) animal skins
   c) animal skins

8.   What singer released his album *Thriller* in 1982?
     Michael Jackson

9.   What era took place between the years 2500 BC
     and 500 BC and is famous for introducing the
     first metal tools and weapons?
     Bronze Age

10. What is the name of the harmful fairies that
     cause destruction on farms and at sea and can
     take many animal forms?
     Púca

Round 4

1. What language is the Book of Kells written in?
   Latin

2. Viking means 'p____ raid' in the Old Norse language.
   Pirate raid

3. What was the Black Death carried by? a) fleas b) mice c) cockroaches
   a) fleas

4. Name the cruel sport, outlawed by Oliver Cromwell, where a dog attacks a chained-up bear.
   Bear-baiting

5. Lord Maguire, Lord O'Neill and Lord O'Donnell, who fought in the Nine Years' War, all had the same first name: a) Harry b) Hugh c) Hector.
   b) Hugh

6. Which of these nationalities were **NOT** Williamites in the Battle of the Boyne? a) English b) French c) Spanish
   c) Spanish

7. The United Irishmen wore normal clothes, sometimes decorated with: a) fur b) feathers c) ribbons.
   c) ribbons

8. What yellow crop did the British Government import from America to try to help during the Great Famine?
   Corn

9. Over how many people were killed in the War of Independence? a) 850 b) 1,000 c) 1,400
   c) 1,400

10. What play by John Millington Synge caused riots during its opening run at the Abbey Theatre? *The P____ of the W____ World.*
    The Playboy of the Western World

Round 5

1. The first-ever broadcast on Irish television was a
    speech by which president?
    Éamon de Valera

2. What is the name of the early Irish alphabet that
    consisted of lines and dots carved on stone?
    Ogham

3. A type of long, loose breeches worn by rich men
    in the 19th century were called: a) plus-threes
    b) plus-fours c) plus-fives.
    b) plus-fours

4. A 'vardo' is a type of: a) wagon b) ship c) train.
    a) wagon

5. Spell 'leprechaun'.
    Leprechaun

6. Which World War began in 1939?
    World War II

7. In what county can you see tracks from a
    tetrapod left in the mud?
    Co. Kerry

8. What is the name of the naughty fairy children
    who sometimes get swapped with human babies?
    Changelings

9. Crop rotation was a farming method introduced by: a) the Normans b) the Celts c) the Vikings.
    a) the Normans

10. What Queen caused a famine in Munster because the people had started a rebellion?
    Queen Elizabeth I

Quiz

9

Round 1

1. A battle fought between the Lord of Fermanagh and the English was named after what food?
   a) cakes b) puddings c) biscuits
   c) biscuits

2. Name the Irish political leader who was known for hating violence: D___ O'C_____.
   Daniel O'Connell

3. True or false: Eoghan Ruadh O'Neill went to Donegal in 1642 to help the British settlers.
   False – he went to help the Ulster Army

4. What were Catholics forbidden from buying during the Penal Laws? a) horses b) land
   c) furniture
   b) land

5. The 1798 rebellion was most successful in what county beginning with 'W'?
   Co. Wexford

6. Michael Collins was born in what county?
   Co. Cork

7. The Troubles lasted for: a) 10 years b) 20 years
   c) 30 years.
   c) 30 years

8. The first version of what famous British flag was designed in 1606?
   Union Jack

9. Who set up the Church of England when the Pope would not end his first marriage? King ____ VIII.
   King Henry VIII

10. Who led the Norman army that landed in 1170? S____.
    Strongbow

Round 2

1. In Celtic clothing, a léine was: a) a tunic b) a skirt
   c) a crown.
   a) a tunic

2. In what Ulster county were two of Ireland's
   biggest dinosaur discoveries made?
   Co. Antrim

3. William Thompson invented the Kelvin scale,
   which measures: a) temperature b) liquid
   c) speed.
   a) temperature

4. Which American president was assassinated in
   1963?
   John F. Kennedy

5. What was the first university in Ireland to allow
   female students? a) University College Dublin
   b) National University of Ireland, Galway
   c) University College Cork
   c) University College Cork

6. What animal feed made from dried grass did the
   Normans introduce?
   Hay

7. A halberd is a type of: a) weapon b) fossil
   c) armour.
   a) weapon

8. The Battle of the Boyne was fought between
    J_____ II and W_____ of Orange.
    James II and William of Orange

9. Wolfe Tone's grave is in what Leinster county?
    Co. Kildare

10. A dord is a musical horn, which is the Irish version
    of what Australian instrument?
    Didgeridoo

Round 3

1. True or false: The cottiers and spailpíns were the wealthiest people during the Great Famine.
   False – they were the poorest

2. RTÉ's first colour broadcast was the _____ ___ Contest.
   Eurovision Song Contest

3. C. S. Lewis is best known for writing *The Chronicles of Narnia*, a series of seven books, including *The ___, the ___ and the _____*.
   The Lion, the Witch and the Wardrobe

4. William Orpen was an artist who painted pictures of scenes from what war?
   World War I

5. Major Walter Gordon Wilson invented the first: a) army tank b) machine gun c) grenade.
   a) army tank

6. What type of megalithic tombs have a giant capstone balanced on at least two entrance stones?
   Portal tombs or dolmens

7. What was the only utensil used for cooking in Celtic times?
   A knife

8. The cure for what disease was found in 1954?
   a) leprosy b) smallpox c) measles
   a) leprosy

9. The remains of what extinct elephant-like animal
   were found in Co. Waterford?
   Woolly mammoth

10. Balor was a Celtic giant who had: a) one big eye
    b) no nose c) four ears.
    a) one big eye

Round 4

1. What is the national emblem of Ireland?
   The harp

2. What was the name of the stepmother in the legend *The Children of Lir*? a) Aoife b) Ava c) Aisling
   a) Aoife

3. Vellum, used to make the pages of the *Book of Kells*, is made from: a) sheepskin b) calfskin c) goatskin.
   b) calfskin

4. To what castle was Robert Emmet marching when his followers started a riot? D____ Castle.
   Dublin Castle

5. Norman people were forbidden from doing which of these acts by the Statutes of Kilkenny? a) marrying an Irish person b) waving at an Irish person c) eating like an Irish person
   a) marrying an Irish person

6. The Battle of the Boyne was fought near what town in Co. Louth?
   Drogheda

7. At which castle did Granuaile insist on staying and always having a place at the dinner table? a) Kilkenny Castle b) Howth Castle c) Slane Castle
   b) Howth Castle

8. Kitchens were set up during the Great Famine to feed what food to the poor?
    Soup

9. True or false: Seamus Heaney won the Nobel Prize for Literature in 1995.
    True

10. Harry Ferguson invented the modern version of what essential farming vehicle?
    Tractor

Round 5

1. 'Wykinglo' is the Norse name for which town?
   Wicklow

2. What colour do leprechauns wear?
   Red

3. Who famously wouldn't move from her seat on a bus in 1955? Rosa _____.
   Rosa Parks

4. The King of Leinster said St Brigid could have as much land as her what could cover? a) hair b) cloak c) dress
   b) cloak

5. True or false: Ireland was once home to spotted hyenas.
   True

6. In what year did the first person land on the moon? a) 1953 b) 1969 c) 1978
   b) 1969

7. Some of the oldest fish traps in Europe were found near Spencer Dock in what county?
   Co. Dublin

8. What is a St Brigid's Cross made from?
   Rushes

9. What was the name for a necklace made from twisted gold worn during the Bronze Age?
   Torc

10. What country was Fionn mac Cumhaill trying to get to when he began building the Giant's Causeway?
    Scotland

Quiz

10

Round 1

1. What type of animal was sent to space for the first time in 1957? a) a dog b) a cat c) a monkey
   a) a dog

2. What plant did St Patrick use to teach the Christian belief of three persons in one God?
   A shamrock

3. The Céide Fields, an example of Neolithic farming, are found in what Connacht county?
   Co. Mayo

4. There is a large statue of which nationalist leader at the bottom of O'Connell Street in Dublin?
   Daniel O'Connell

5. In Celtic clothing, what was a crios? a) a shirt b) a belt c) shoes
   b) a belt

6. Brian Boru was killed at the Battle of C____.
   Battle of Clontarf

7. Aengus was the god of a) war b) love c) time.
   b) love

8. True or false: High Crosses were used as grave markers.
   False – they were status symbols

9. In what Leinster county did the Normans land in 1169?
    Co. Wexford

10. What was the name of the area that Henry VII took control of? The P___.
    The Pale

Round 2

1. Wolfe Tone tried to land at what bay with 14,000 French soldiers? a) Bantry Bay b) Clew Bay c) Donegal Bay
   a) Bantry Bay

2. What county did English forces first attack in the Nine Years' War? a) Fermanagh b) Tyrone c) Donegal
   a) Fermanagh

3. Which of these was NOT one of the activities banned by Oliver Cromwell? a) going to the theatre b) drinking alcohol c) eating chocolate
   c) eating chocolate

4. William was the Prince of Orange in: a) Germany b) Holland c) France.
   b) Holland

5. What type of writing did John Robert Gregg invent that was widely used by secretaries to take speedy notes?
   Shorthand

6. Robert Emmet was arrested and imprisoned at K_____ Gaol in Dublin.
   Kilmainham Gaol

7. Daniel O'Connell's face was on the old a) £10 note b) £20 note c) £50 note.
   b) £20 note

8. The Society of St V_____ de _____ was set up during the famine to distribute food to the poor.
    St Vincent de Paul

9. The James Joyce novel *Ulysses* is set on 16 June 1904. This day is now known as what?
    Bloomsday

10. In ancient Ireland, communities held a festival called an aonach, usually at the same time as an important: a) funeral b) wedding c) birth.
    a) funeral

Round 3

1. A flannel or cotton collarless shirt is often called: a) a mother shirt b) a grandad shirt c) a brother shirt.
    b) a grandad shirt

2. In early national schools, children learned to write using: a) pen and paper b) parchment and quill c) slates and chalk.
    c) slates and chalk

3. Spell 'suffragettes'.
    Suffragettes

4. What Irish television channel was founded in 1961?
    RTÉ

5. You can visit the *Dunbrody* famine ship in New Ross, Co. _____.
    Wexford

6. What type of megalithic tomb has a courtyard in front of the main entrance?
    Court tomb

7. A gorget is a type of: a) clothing b) jewellery c) armour.
    b) jewellery

8. What province is named after King Conn Céadchathach?
    Connacht

9. What was the colour of the bull that Queen
    Maeve stole from Cúchulainn?
    Brown

10. What date is St Patrick's Day?
    17 March

Round 4

1. Leading up to the 1798 Rebellion, what province was the one area of Ireland where Catholics and Protestants had joined together?
   Ulster

2. What is another name for the Christian group the Society of Friends?
   Quakers

3. Daniel O'Connell was nicknamed 'The L_____' because he achieved Catholic emancipation.
   The Liberator

4. What was the name of Fionn mac Cumhaill's teacher, who caught the Salmon of Knowledge?
   a) Fergal b) Finnegas c) Fintan
   b) Finnegas

5. Which of the following is NOT a deadly disease from the time of the Great Famine? a) typhus b) cholera c) cooties
   c) cooties

6. The first cinema in Ireland was established by the writer J___ J____.
   James Joyce

7. The Beaufort Scale, invented by Francis Beaufort, measures: a) earthquakes b) wind c) rain.
   b) wind

8. Ghillies are a type of: a) dancing shoe b) work
   trousers c) reading glasses.
   a) dancing shoe

9. What red-haired puppet was born in 1979?
   Bosco

10. Who became the Queen of England in 1952
    and is the longest-reigning monarch in British
    history?
    Queen Elizabeth II

Round 5

1. King Conn Céadchathach is said to have fought how many battles? a) one hundred b) one thousand c) one million
   a) one hundred

2. What song competition did Ireland enter for the first time in 1965?
   Eurovision Song Contest

3. Who was the first female president of Ireland?
   Mary Robinson

4. What type of free school was introduced in 1967? a) free primary school b) free secondary school c) free third-level college
   Free secondary school

5. Name the conflict between Unionists and Nationalists in Northern Ireland that lasted from 1968–1998.
   The Troubles

6. What province led a rebellion against Queen Elizabeth in 1580?
   Munster

7. King Cormac mac Airt died when he choked on the bone of what type of fish?
   Salmon

8. What were the earliest Norman castles made from?
    Wood

9. What Leinster county was formerly named King's
    County by Queen Mary I?
    Co. Offaly

10. Wexford was declared a republic in 1798, which
    lasted for: a) three days b) three weeks c) three
    months.
    b) three weeks